I'm An Aspie

*A Poetic Memoir for Living the Human Experience
Through the Eyes of Asperger's*

Brian R. King LCSW

Forward by: Temple Grandin

1st WORLD
PUBLISHING

I'm An Aspie

A Poetic Memoir for Living the Human Experience
Through the Eyes of Asperger's

Brian R. King LCSW

© Brian R. King 2008

Published by 1stWorld Publishing
P.O. Box 2211 Fairfield, Iowa 52556
tel: 641-209-5000 • fax: 641-209-3001
web: www.1stworldpublishing.com

First Edition

LCCN: 2008935228
SoftCover ISBN: 978-1-4218-9023-4
HardCover ISBN: 978-1-4218-9003-6
eBook ISBN: 978-1-4218-9024-1

This material has been written and published solely for educational purposes. The author and the publisher shall have neither liability nor responsibility to any person or entity with respect to any loss, damage or injury caused or alleged to be caused directly or indirectly by the information contained in this book.

*This book is dedicated to those who love me
just the way I am. For those who don't,
you don't know what you're missing.*

Acknowledgements

There are more people to thank for helping me arrive at this point in my life than I can possibly mention. I need to thank my Dad for giving me the gift of my unique neurological heritage. I thank my Mom for always helping me walk to the beat of my own drummer when the rest of the world was telling me not to.

I need to thank Susan Moreno (founder of MAAP **www.maapservices.org**) for allowing me to attend the annual MAAP conference a few years ago and participate in several panel discussions. The opportunity to share my ideas with a large audience in this way did much to move my professional career along. The best thing to come from the MAAP experience was that it caught the attention of Michael John Carley, the Executive Director of GRASP (**www.grasp.org**). MJ invited me into the GRASP family as the facilitator of one of it's support groups and it has been nothing but progress ever since. MJ has been a selfless mentor and has served as a tremendous role model in helping hone my own skills in the subtle art of diplomacy.

MJ also did me the tremendous honor of connecting me with Temple Grandin. Temple in turn graciously agreed to take the time to read this book and share her thoughts which have become the forward to this book.

Special thanks to Annette Becklund LCSW (**www.AnnetteLBecklund.com**), Kris Lonsway Ph.D (**www.LonswayConsulting.com**), and Sue Moreno, M.A,.A.B.S. who offered many wonderful suggestions for refining the language in many aspects of this book. Last but not least I need to thank my boys. They are a daily source of inspiration and compel my continued work to help create a world they will be welcomed into with open arms and where their differences with be embraced with gratitude instead of rejected with distain. Thank you to everyone for all that you do to help me become a better me.

Forward

I really like Brian's positive approach to Asperger's. There is a great need in the Autism/Asperger community for more positive thinking. There needs to be a lot more emphasis on the person's area of strength. People on the spectrum have uneven skills. They are often good at one thing and bad at another. Too often the educational emphasis is put on the deficits, instead of building up the area of strength.

When I was a child my ability in art was nurtured. I was given a book on perspective drawing and all kinds of art activities were encouraged. My abilities with visual thinking and drawing helped me to be successful in my career of designing livestock handling facilities. Parents and teachers need to find each individual's area of strength and build it up. I have observed that there are three types of specialized Autistic/Asperger thinking. They are:

1. Visual Thinkers like me who think in photo realistic pictures. My weak area in algebra and foreign language.

2. Pattern thinkers who see patterns in numbers and music. These people are often good at computer programming and engineering. Their area of weakness is often reading.

3. Word Fact Thinkers who are good at having vast knowledge

of facts about their favorite subject. They are not visual thinkers.

I hope that the writings of Brian King will help Aspies every-where to look on the positive side.

Temple Grandin, Author

Thinking in Pictures

CONTENTS

Introduction

I learned that Asperger's was a large part of who I am when my oldest son Zach entered first grade. Amongst other things he began demonstrating extreme difficulty with transitions, unexpected changes and would panic when the class schedule wasn't followed as planned.

Half way into the school year his anxiety reached a point where the teacher was unable to support him on her own. She phoned me one day to discuss her observations and her suspicions that Zach was somewhere on the Autism Spectrum. I was shocked as I hadn't observed the characteristics she was reporting. I had to admit that Zach didn't experience the kinds of demands at home that school places upon him which would explain this.

I became impatient with the slow pace of the school's testing process and took him to our pediatrician. That led to a referral to a Clinical Psychologist and an Occupational Therapist. It was in filling out the paperwork specific to Asperger's that I began seeing much of myself in the questions on the page.

I went through my own crisis of identity as I absorbed this information about myself. It literally allowed me to rewrite my past which was filled with memories of bullying and rejection from peers and adults alike. A life of social clumsiness and finding the larger world both fascinating and confusing. These and a host of sensory sensitivities I'd always had and wasn't aware varied so dramatically from how others experience the world.

It also shed light on a major turning point in my life which I believe being an Aspie helped me survive. As I write these words I am celebrating my 20th year cancer free. I wrote about my experience of surviving cancer in a book called *What To Do When You're Totally Screwed*. Though I wrote it long before learning of my Asperger's, the strategies contained in that book are very useful for Aspies (someone living the Asperger's Experience) and Neurotypicals (the average person) alike.

In short, being diagnosed with cancer at age 18 turned my life upside down as a diagnosis of an aggressive cancer thrust me into full scale chaos which included surgery, chemotherapy and the loss of friends who couldn't handle watching me go through such a difficult experience.

Feeling so out of control and being in so much pain caused me to go through periods or rage, depression, panic and thoughts of suicide. I finally reached a point where I was sick of the emotional rollercoaster that no one seemed able to help me get out of. It was then that I decided to take control back.

Like many Aspies I live in my intellect so that's where I went. I knew that my mind was filled with angry thoughts one moment and depressing thoughts the next. Though some say I was simply going through the grieving process, it seemed to me that I was stuck in it. I went to the public library and began reading every book on psychology, philosophy and self-help I could find.

In eastern philosophy I found the thoughts that would gain me the kind of control over my mind that I was looking for. I used my Aspergian tendency toward hyperfocus to completely immerse myself in practicing this unique way of thinking until I had gotten control of my mind back.

It was going through this process that helped me develop a

deep and thorough insight into my own mind and thought processes that has come to serve me well in the field of Asperger's. After I learned that Zach and I were Aspies I began attending parent groups to find support for myself. I was surprised when parents began turning to me for insight into their children.

It turned out that I understood myself so well that in talking about my own experiences I was able to help them understand their own children in a way nobody else ever could.

They kept telling me that my perspective was uniquely positive in focusing on what a person has to work with that can help him lead a productive life where he can do the most with what he's got. It is my position that it isn't the size of the contribution you make to the world that makes you valuable, it only matters that your contribution is positive.

Too often parents, teachers, professionals, employers, you name it tend to emphasize and criticize what they don't like about a person and what they want to see changed. I used to work for a man who refused to offer compliments to anyone. He said "no news is good news" and "if I don't talk to you it means you're doing your job." How patently ridiculous is this logic? He was essentially saying that the moment I'm doing something wrong is the only time he feels I'm worthy of his attention. How the heck am I supposed to know what the right way is if no one ever tells me when I'm doing it? In his mind positivity is the absence of negative feedback.

This unfortunately is the story of many lives whether on the Autism Spectrum or not. Too many people walking around upset and complaining about what's missing in their lives. They spend so much energy being dissatisfied that after awhile the first thing they see is what's missing. This is never more damaging than when all they can see is what's missing in those around them or even worse in themselves.

I thought this way for the longest time before the depression

I experienced during cancer taught me that the more I focused on what I didn't want the more of it I saw because it was what I was giving all of my attention to. A game has never been won by focusing on how not to lose, it's always by focusing on how to win.

Once I learned that lesson I was able to start living from a perspective of only looking for what works instead of what's broken. To look at the flowers instead of the weeds. How can you commit to building your strengths if you're giving all of your attention to your challenges? It's like covering your eyes and asking "Why is it so dark?"

One of the best examples of my positive approach to Asperger's is in how I define it. When I ask my clients what Asperger's means to them I've heard answers such as "It means I have a disability" or "It means I can't do things." The same people who taught them to view Asperger's that way are the people that are responsible for preparing them to make their contribution in the world. They've begun by encouraging their children to approach life with the mantra "I think I can't, I think I can't." The story of the little engine that couldn't.

When I first learned what Asperger's meant as the world defined it, with words such as Syndrome, Disorder, Disability, I immediately concluded that this was a point of view which offered nothing to me or my children and provided me nothing with which I could possibly build my life on. It is this attitude that led me to say, what do I do with this that will allow me to be better as a result of it?

As I got to know myself and my son as Aspies I developed a definition that was balanced and more reflective of a human being with a unique set of strengths as challenges. My definition of Asperger's is simply this: *the dominance of specialized thinking and ability that prioritizes doing one task, one way, one step at a time with limited flexibility. This occurs to various degrees and results in strengths in the areas of focus (especially in the area of specialization), honesty, detail orientation, logic and original thinking. This tendency toward specialization also often results in challenges developing more generalized and complex skill sets such as conventional socialization and communication.* To simplify this even further would be to describe Asperger's as "A Specialized Way of Being." If you're interested in the more clinical, deficit based definition of Asperger's you can search the internet for "DSM IV Asperger's."

The more I shared my perspective the more I was asked to write what I know in a book of some sort. Well here it is, my contribution to the growing body of published works on the subject of Asperger's and the human experience. Please let it be known that the process of writing this has been at times exhilarating, exhausting, frustrating and self defeating. This was primarily because I was trying to write the book other people told me needed to be written. "People need solutions" they would always say.

I did my best to write as I'd seen others write and it wasn't a comfortable experience. I wasn't enjoying it at all because the way I was trying to make myself write wasn't natural to me. I am not a fluid thinker who can assemble thoughts in a sequential way. I am a tangential thinker. I think in moments, in bullet points, in bursts of inspiration. I can also become redundant, repeat myself, write or say something over and over again the same way. You know I can keep going after making my point, just keep repeating what I've already said. Get the point?

The insights people have found so valuable from me came in the moment in response to unique problems and questions they posed. They didn't come from a storehouse of knowledge in the front of my mind that I had ready access to when I sat down to write. In short, I don't know what I know until you ask me a question.

When I finally sat down to begin writing I agonized for months over what to put on these pages. I wanted to offer something unique to the public discourse regarding what it's like to live the Asperger's experience in a solution focused way.

Stories of growing up misunderstood and mistreated have been written by many so it makes no sense for me to write another. At a loss for what to write I was about to give up until I realized that I was doing myself a tremendous disservice by thinking that anything I wrote had to follow any standard set of rules regarding what a book should be or how it should be written. I also realized that I needed to allow myself to not take so much responsibility for writing a book that was spectacular but instead to just write sincerely and openly then let you decide what in this book is useful for you.

One commonality to those with Asperger's is a special interest or area of specialization. Mine is an insatiable interest in thought patterns and processes. People often tell me I think too much. In my world it's my favorite activity and examining my own thinking has resulted in my becoming better and better at it. It is this interest that has led to the insights you will begin reading shortly.

I thought about the kind of writing I could do. I wanted to look forward to writing and take pride in the result. My first love in writing is poetry. It is also the greatest reflection of who I am and how I think. I am at my core a hopeless romantic and a philosopher and my poetry reflects that better than any article I've ever written. My poems are long enough to make a point and short enough for me to keep my thoughts together. Therefore it made sense for me to write a book that would allow me to communicate the best way I know how.

So here is my book, a poetic memoir of my philosophical reflections on life. Though it is written in poetic form it's overall theme can be considered one of mindset. A particular frame of mind for creating a particular kind of perspective that leads to a particular kind of life. It may contain everything, something or only a few things you need. I'll do the best I can to provide information that is useful for you. Please do your best to take away what's useful in this book instead of being critical for what you feel is missing. Asperger's often creates more questions than any one book can answer anyway.

All that I have written in these pages reflects my ongoing effort to find deeper meaning in all that I experience. I've organized the poems alphabetically for the sake of structure not as a means of creating a sense of flow in the content. This structure also demonstrates that I don't view my life as a fluid narrative but more as a series of snapshots, scenes, or vibrant moments in time. Therefore what I present here is a collection of powerful moments, observations and memorable lessons from my life. I hope you enjoy them, learn from them, share them and discuss them.

Abundance

I look into the sky each morn
With gratitude for being born.
I face the day after a good night's rest
Determined to give my very best.

I prepare this day with an energized soul
And a focus on a worthwhile goal.
I always keep one thing in mind.
What I don't have now I am destined to find.

For I drink from a cup that is overflowing.
Filled from a stream that is never slowing.
A spirit that soars to touch the sky.
A river so deep it will never dry.

My glass is not half empty
Nor is it half full as you can see
It shows what I have so far gained
And the journey before me that still remains.

If I live a life of scarcity
A lack of things is what I see.
Then life will always be so tough.
With the fear that I don't have enough.

When thinking there is nothing more
It's time to open another door.
Then before my eyes what I will see
Is another opportunity.

I am born into abundance
To help me go the distance.
Having everything I need to live
I always have everything to give.

Inspired by a second chance at life and all the opportunities that follow.

The Art of Forgiveness

There are many different tasks in life
One of the hardest for seeing through
Is when having been wronged by another
Forgiveness is asked of you.

There are those who ask forgiveness
After committing a hurtful slight
With the intention that their wrong
Will somehow become right.

Some believe to give forgiveness
Is an act of clemency.
When in their heart it's payback
That they'd really like to see.

Forgiveness is none of the above
Now for a big surprise.
The art of true forgiveness
Is in where your focus lies.

Those who focus on the act,
The betrayal and the pain.
Are committed to the effort
Of helping anger to remain.

Inside every painful experience
Something valuable resides.
A seed of potential growth
Through the lesson it provides.

So the art of true forgiveness
Is commitment to the lesson.
A quite useful perspective
That helps the pain to lessen.

When you focus on the benefit
Instead of bitterness and pain.
You walk away with gratitude
And a wisdom that remains.

Inspired by the peace experienced from releasing your painful past.

The Bending Of The Tree

Before the wind the tree is still.
It is calm and silent without a frill.
From the oncoming wind it does not hide.
With the winds of the past it does not abide.

Whenever there is present a breeze or a gust
The tree's only inclination is to simply adjust.
It seeks not to resist the wind or to give up and be subdued.
It patiently adjusts until the adversity concludes.

The tree does not resist the wind to demonstrate its brawn
Adversity is temporary, and the wind will soon be gone.
It does not overreact to breezes with an excessive bend
Only to wind that is there will the bending branches attend.

Life is a neverending change from gentle breeze to gust.
To which the spontaneity of the tree will continually adjust.
Adversity is not positive nor is it an evil wretch
But one of many changes that require my branches to stretch.

The tree lives in the present with what is actually here
Winds of the future or of the past the tree will never fear.
It sits in peace without a sound and if the wind should blow
It will adjust accordingly then allow the wind to go.

The tree is not resentful or inconvenienced by the breeze
Nor is it wishful for a life that is lead with greater ease.
Wishing for the wind to differ does not change what is real
That which actually is I must ultimately deal.

Adjusting as I must
To any degree of breeze or gust.
As the breeze and bend subsides
At the peace of the moment I can finally arrive.

The resilience of the tree does not belong to it I see.
This simple wisdom is inherent in all the things that be.
To live in peace I will look within so I can clearly see
I, too, embody the patient resilience practiced by the tree.

Inspired by the importance of flexibility and adapting to change whenever possible.

The Blame Game

Tag you're it; it's all your fault
Yet another of life's unfair assaults.
Another injustice I'm forced to face
I lose again in this lifelong race.

I'm only this way cause of how I was raised.
It's my parent's fault for not giving more praise.
I'm not the problem, it's you not me,
For I am a helpless victim you see.

I would like to change but I am unable
I have a disorder that makes me disabled.
I can't change this is just who I am,
If you don't like it go ahead and scram.

However, my hand seems to be getting sore
As my finger pointing increases more and more.
If I don't figure out another way to proceed
My future holds little prospect indeed.

Perhaps if the finger pointing away from me
Was turned in the direction of who I choose to be.
Is it possible that things could finally change
When my perception is rearranged?

My dreams and I had been kept apart
Until the day that I and blame did part,
Because I discovered deep in my heart
That it was all on me from the very start.

Inspired by the paralysis of blame many Aspies indulge in and the power and freedom that comes with personal responsibility.

Certifiable

I received my badge of honor today
In exchange for a job well done.
A certificate that allows me to say
Fellow Aspies I am one.

I have successfully passed the test
That makes my suspicions true.
I am somewhat different from all the rest
An Aspie through and through.

I can hold up my degree with pride
And show others what I've achieved
Any doubt can now subside
Through this certificate I've received.

With no unanswered question
Will my time be occupied.
My life now has a new direction
Now that I'm certified.

Inspired by the importance of looking at Asperger's as a Certification instead of a diagnosis. There is no sense of pride in receiving a diagnosis but there is in receiving a certification.

People can be professionally certified in something and discuss it with a sense of accomplishment. Their certificate shows they've satisfied the necessary requirements to earn their certificate. It is more a recognition of an Aspie's unique gifts rather than their unique challenges. It also celebrates what they have to offer instead of what they need to fix.

When you think about it people have to meet certain requirements to be Aspies so why not call it a certification instead of a diagnosis? A certification denotes what a person is able to do right. A diagnosis says what a person has difficulty or is unable to do. A diagnosis is like the anti-diploma. Let's make Asperger's a certification in a unique branch of eccentricity and then the world can celebrate our accomplishments along side us.

A Choice

Today I made a simple choice
To heed the will of my inner voice.

It said embrace your deepest dream
And let that be your life long theme.

I choose to live by the strength of belief
And not by the fear that is freedom's thief.

I choose to love who I choose to love
Ignoring the scrutiny of the social white glove.

I choose to embrace those who bring out my best
And to repel those who fill my life with unrest.

I choose only the thoughts that empower my vision
Being true to myself with my every decision.

I have the choice to make a choice
To scream at the top of my lungs and rejoice.

Rejoice for the person I have become
And to the apology I owe to no one.

I am true to myself without compromise
It would be wrong for me to do otherwise.

Inspired by the most powerful human ability in existence. The power to make a choice about what you will think, say and do at every moment. Those choices are what create your life. If you don't like your life then examine your choices. Then, choose to do otherwise.

Contents Of The Leaf

I experience the leaf as it sits upon the tree.
For there lies the universe before me.
A symphony of interdependence
Being played in this very moment.

Can I see the sun in the leaf
As it penetrates the green?
Giving rise to the birth of the leaf.
Giving rise to the nourishment of the leaf.
Giving rise to the growth of the leaf.

Without the sun means without the leaf.
The leaf is part sun.
The leaf is a manifestation of sunlight.
The leaf and sun are one.
Yes. I can see the sun in the leaf.

Can I see the ocean in the leaf?
As the ocean becomes the cloud
The water is carried across the tree-covered lands.
The tree is nourished as it is bathed in life-giving rains.
The leaf is nourished by the water.
Yes. I can see the ocean in the leaf.

Can I see the universe in the leaf?
Without sun without cloud.
Without cloud without rain.
Without rain without nourishment of the earth.
Without leaf.
The leaf is because the sun is.
The leaf is because the earth is.
The leaf is because the ocean is.

The leaf is not just a leaf.
It is sun, earth, and ocean.
It does not exist as itself.
It cannot exist as itself.
It exists as the universe.
It only looks like a leaf.
The universe is the leaf.
Within the leaf lies the universe.
Yes. I can see the universe in the leaf.
Yes. I can see myself in the leaf
I can see the universe in myself.
I can see the universe is myself.

Inspired by the interdependence of all things, especially Aspies and Non-Aspies. There is a place for everything and everyone under the sun. We rely upon each other, we contribute to each other's lives. We each do our part to make society evolve and become better. One important lesson Aspies have to teach is that there are many ways to be human.

Equality

The ideal skin is not white
Because the ideal day is partly night.
The sky is not always blue.
It often has a contrasting hue.

There cannot be an ideal race
Because everything has got its place.
Just because one thinks he is the best.
Does not mean he is above the rest.

An ego that is ten feet tall
Makes him feel above it all.
Some think to do the best they can do
Means they must step all over you.

The only way they can be right
Is through intimidation, violence, and fright.
They are not the champions of truth
They are the deceivers of me and you.

With angry emotions running high
It's do what they say or die.
Hate is evil's reflection
A spiritual infection

Moving us in the wrong direction.
It's a moral defection
A fear and greed connection
That needs some serious correction.

To have peace among each race
All things must have their place.
If this truth is not realized
We will continue to hasten our own demise.

Inspired by the divisiveness between us all and our senseless need to seek new ways to separate from each other. Whether it be racial, social, political, religious etc., history has always shown that division causes pain and cooperation causes healing and joy.

Expectation

With expectation comes impatience
When I desire things my way.
For nature's agenda does not parallel my own
But embraces the rhythm of the day.

With expectation comes anger
When things do not turn out as planned.
Because I don't trust nature to itself
But wish it to be at my command.

With expectation comes selfishness
When I expect to get all I want.
Seeking value in further acquisition
I ignore the value in what I've got.

With expectation comes intolerance.
When I expect that I am correct.
I often base judgment of others
On perceptions that are suspect.

With expectation comes disappointment
When I anticipate tomorrow.
Because I forget to concern myself with this day
Which determines the manner of those that follow.

With expectation comes dissatisfaction
Always expecting something more grand.
Until I realize that the sunshine's brightest
Upon the place in which I stand.

But with acceptance I find peace
When I let day pass into night.
As the universe has done for eons now
And continues to do it right.

Inspired by our need to impose our will and be in control at all times. When it comes down to it the only control we have is self-control. When we master that, life's unpredictability can be easier to manage.

Eye To Eye

"Look at me" is your request
When I look away from you.
Insisting that I listen best
When eye contact ensues.

You think that if I look away
Your words I am dismissing.
But if I don't let my eyes stray
Your words I will be missing.

To think I listen with my eyes
Just simply isn't true.
To listen you must realize
Is what ears are used to do.

Many people will suggest
That eye contact is a must.
Without it you they will reject
As someone they can trust.

I wish to make this very clear
I say this under oath.
I can look or I can hear
But I cannot do both.

My brain just doesn't work that way
I can look or listen to you.
I can focus better on what you say
When I do one instead of two.

Not to look you in the eye
Will not keep us apart.
I don't need to look in your eye
To see into your heart.

Inspired of course by the fact that communication is a complex process that can't be derailed or belittled by something as little as the absence of eye contact. Many Aspies including myself find it difficult to look and listen at the same time. So ask yourself whether you prefer to be looked at or listened to. I think the choice is obvious.

Experience 101

There is a single course of study
From which no one graduates.
On a moment to moment basis
Our performance fluctuates.

This course is from the school of life,
It is called Experience 101.
What we learn and what we don't
Determines who we can become.

When you flunk this class you suffer,
But not from a failing grade.
You suffer the loss of opportunity
From the choice you could have made.

Still others choose a course of action
With an often unwanted effect.
They repeat the pattern over again,
But frustration is all they collect.

It has been said that when one expects
New effect with the same causality.
You have the most compelling evidence
Of your very own insanity.

If this is the case with yourself or another
Then something is clearly amiss.
Experience is trying to teach you
While the lesson you resist.

You must listen to experience
Or the class you will not pass.
You haven't moved to the next level
If a difficulty continues to last.

It can often be quite painful but
Learning from experience has much benefit.
Remember there is something far more painful
When you never learn from it.

As with a later poem called "School of Life," this is a reflection on the value and power of learning from your experiences.

Failproof

What in life would you dare to do
If you knew you couldn't fail?
To never come in second place
But always to prevail.

This is an important point to consider
And of your answers please keep track.
Because they reveal where fear of failure
Is the thing that holds you back.

When avoiding all the negatives
Becomes more important to you,
You tend to avoid the risk of success
And safety is what you pursue.

But let's assume for a moment
That our original premise is true.
That it's actually possible not to fail,
In that case what would you do?

Would you find yourself taking more risks
And seeing more things through?
Would you suddenly be dreaming bigger?
What exactly would you do?

When you focus on the outcome
You're far less likely to quit.
Because you look beyond the failure
To success you can commit.

Often a simple shift in focus
Is all it really takes.
To create the winning mindset
And keep you always in first place.

Inspired by the fact that those that succeed in life are driven by the conviction that success is inevitable and simply a matter of time. Achieving what they do because they realize that their goal is more important than fear.

Free Will

With a handful of clouds God lined the sky.
Then added wind that they might fly.

God assembled pieces of Earth side by side.
Then watched as those pieces began to slide.

God created the rivers and let them flow.
Then watched as they filled the oceans below.

Then God created humankind,
With compassionate hearts and curious minds.

God looked at his creation from up above
And wanted to see what it was capable of.

So with the flick of a finger and a resounding voice.
He instilled in all creation the gift of choice.

God was extremely surprised that day
When creation chose to act in a curious way.

The wind spun the clouds with a deafening sound
As a funnel shaped torrent slammed to the ground.

The oceans did swell with a cyclonic din.
Which would saturate the shore then calm again.

The Earth began to shift and shake
As the rest of creation could feel the quake.

Humankind began to weep and moan
When some of their members turned on their own.

But soon the skies did clear again
The seas did calm the Earth settled in.

Man decided to embrace one another
In the largest family of sisters and brothers.

For all of creation has choices to make.
The oceans can surge and the Earth can quake.

But we as people can rise above.
And grow from our choices with courage and love.

Inspired by the fact that the world and people around us often seem to be in a state of chaos, sometimes choosing to compete and sabotage each other, but are also capable of working together which historically has led to greater prosperity and beauty in the world. I wish our leaders would see what is possible by working together instead of against each other.

The Future I Set

I believe in my life in progress
And in learning from the past.
I see life as an evolving drama
A biography of its cast.

My future is more than the sum effect
Of the causes from my past.
I believe that things can always improve.
Which allows my dreams to last.

My children stand upon my shoulders
And see the road that lies ahead.
I must show them a future beaming with hope
Not a path they should fear to tread.

Each choice is a brick in the road of my life
Each lesson the concrete that holds them tight.
I must continue to learn in order to grow.
The taller I grow the further my sight.

As I build a future that exceeds my past
I will only truly succeed
By keeping in mind the example I set
For those who follow my lead.

The best hope I have for the time to come
Is to know I'm better than what I am shown.
And no matter what the choices of others
I still have choices of my own.

Inspired again not only by the power of choice, but by the example we each set for those around us by the choices we make. I have set a very high standard for myself. This often results in my being very hard on myself and feeling exhausted as I continue to push myself to measure up to my own standards. I also do so because the goals I've set for myself are necessary to accomplish if I expect to see a more accepting world for myself, my children and my fellow Aspies.

The Hidden Light

I take a moment and close my eyes
To take a deep, long look inside.
I see that images begin to rise
Of everything I choose to hide.

So how much strength does it require
To keep my truth contained?
Am I afraid if I light my fire
No excuses will remain?

Will I continue to go along
And put my dreams aside?
At what point did I learn it wrong
To mount my dreams and ride?

Like the song of joyful morning birds
Like the river waters glisten
The best in me is beyond mere words
So I must quietly sit and listen.

I allow my mind to become still
And engage in deep reflection
With the possible my mind does fill
So I can move in that direction.

No longer will I continue to lose
By embracing deep self-doubt.
Sustaining one more inner bruise
As my light fights to get out.

So I choose to embrace my inner light
And finally let it shine.
Then the world will experience a shorter night
And in me see the divine.

Inspired by the ongoing effort of many to pressure Aspies to hold it together, stop being themselves and pretend to be who they are not. They do not realize they're forcing Aspies to live lives of quiet desperation. To live in fear of being themselves out of concern that they will be abandoned for being different. I strongly encourage Aspies to come together however they can and through supporting each other learn to relish and respect what is beautiful about themselves and worthy of sharing with the world. Through their new found confidence the world will have the opportunity to embrace yet another color in the spectrum of humankind.

I Had A God

Before I was born I had a God
With very much to teach.
And slowly he prepared me
For what he was about to preach.

He first gave me a body
A fragile one at best;
To serve as a special vessel
For all that would come next.

He placed inside my body
A warm and beating heart.
He then filled it with all his love
But that was just the start.

He placed two ears upon my head
To listen beyond his words.
Because the truth of what he says
Goes beyond what can be heard.

He then gave me the gift of eyes
But not for simple sight.
He encouraged me to have a vision
That surpasses the black and white.

Encased within my head a brain
Along with a powerful mind.
To receive the flow of experience
That my perception may be refined.

When I was born I had a God
Who gave to me a choice.
To walk the path as I saw fit
Or to listen to his voice.

But God presented a unique challenge
Not always speaking with his voice
But through a series of teachers
Whom I followed was purely my choice.

Some would lead me to his glory
Others to his wrath.
God had endless faith in me
And my choice to walk his path.

For whenever I would go astray
And head in the wrong direction.
My God would extend a gentle hand
And slap me to attention.

As I grew up I had a God
Who lent me many a gift.
A multitude of talents
That I might inspire and uplift.

For the greatest gift that I received
Is a uniquely human perk,
The honor and the privilege
To be an instrument of his work.

As I continued to be his humble student
I also began to guide.
Helping others to discover
Their talents locked inside.

As I grew old I had a God
Who sent many people my way.
To express their thanks for all I'd done
During my brief but meaningful stay.

As my eyes began to close
I had a God to see me through
He gave me the gift of peace and comfort
For all I helped him do.

When I died I had a God
Who took me by the hand
Who shared with me a special secret
That I now could understand.

The life that I'd been given to live
Was merely preparation
For the role that I was destined to play
In this final destination.

God bestowed upon me angel's wings
To guide others as they begin,
To walk the path of preparation
Toward the place that I am in.

Inspired not by an endorsement of religious belief but more by the need to convince myself that the struggles of life have a point. That no matter what happens in my life it's going to get me somewhere. It's also inspired by the fact that if God is infallible then Aspies must be on purpose. We are here to contribute our part to the grand design that is God's work. Last time I checked, there is no commandment that reads "Thou shall be normal."

If You Need Me

If you ever need a shoulder
On which to have a cry.
Pick one of my two, either will do
I'll be happy to bring it by.

If all you need is a friendly ear
I would love to hear you talk.
If you wish to wander the town all day
We can take a little walk.

When it seems that you can take no more
And you're unable to maintain.
I'll lend you my back to ease the load,
And my heart to ease the pain.

If ever the need to call arrives
Anytime of night or day.
Whether sound asleep or sick with flu,
I will never turn you away.

Whenever you're consumed with rage
And want to tear out all your hair.
Don't sacrifice your beautiful mane
I have a plethora to spare.

If ever you need me, anytime,
Just call and I'll be there.
I'll be at your side without condition,
Anytime and anywhere.

Inspired by the unconditional love I've received from some very special people in my life. Primarily my mother. It's this kind of support that has made the intolerable experiences of life survivable. It's also what is needed in helping Aspies navigate a world that at present doesn't offer this kind of support to them. Those who can provide it will be granting a gift with a value that cannot be described in words.

I Shall Be The Sun

The horizon slowly opens for dawn
As sunshine awakens the day.
The blanket of darkness is slowly withdrawn
So life can get underway.

The rays of sunshine encompass all things.
Nothing they touch is rejected.
All things beautiful, ugly, a burden, a blessing
With compassion all are accepted.

The nurturing sunlight embraces all life
On no preference does it dwell.
It embraces equally the accord and strife
No attempts are made to quell.

I am grateful to the sun
For the life it helps create.
The business of life can be easily done
From a warmth that permeates.

It holds not an inquisition
Of what is worthy of its shine.
The sun makes no decision
Of what's allowed in the grand design.

The sun helps provide a place in which
Things can simply be as they are.
Where all things can freely find their niche
And their true nature will not be marred.

The sun is not eclipsed by fear.
It allows itself and others to shine.
The eye of sunshine is crystal clear
And so shall this eye be mine.

Radiating strength that is shared with others
Under this blanket of acceptance all are one.
I shall live with all my sisters and brothers.
I shall be the sun.

Inspired by the fact that on its grandest level the universe models inclusion and acceptance. If only we were to pay better attention.

I'm An Aspie

Allow me to introduce me to you
I'm someone quite unique.
To tell everything would take an hour or two
So I'll give you a little peek.

For me the light is far too bright
Some smells are far too strong.
Some touches are far too light
Still I manage to get along.

My interests are but one or two
And that's enough for me.
I have some friends but very few
Just the way I like it to be.

I see life in a special way
Though I'm often misunderstood.
I know that every single day
I'm doing the world some good.

I may talk a little different than you
Still I have a lot to say.
I may not like the things you do.
I like to do things my own way.

Though I get right to the point
I don't mean to offend.
Though I hate to disappoint
I'd like to hurry toward the end.

I prefer to spend my time alone
It's easier that way.
In solitude my brilliance is shone
So a loner I will stay.

Sometimes I seek the company of friends
If there's something to talk about
And when the conversation ends
I'll find my own way out.

I wasn't created in order to fit
I may push when you choose to pull.
Though I'm different you must admit
I keep life from becoming dull.

The myths of what makes others the norm
I hope one day to shatter
I'm here to institute sweeping reform
That's one reason that I matter.

Please learn to love me for who I am
And not who you want me to be.
I'm open to what I can learn from you
But you also must learn from me.

I think this one speaks for itself.

The Lighthouse

I am like the lighthouse
And you are the ship at sea.
I shine my beacon of light upon you
Through all adversity.

When the waters beneath you are churning
And tossing you about.
I will cast my beam upon you
To assist you in your bout.

I will keep my light upon you
So you always know I'm there.
This struggle on the rugged sea
Is something we both share.

When the path ahead is clouded
By a fog as thick as oil.
I'll guide you to a clearing
And through all of this turmoil.

I'll keep you safe from harm
From a shore that's riddled with rock.
I'll lead you through the waters
So you can safely dock.

When you venture upon your journey once more
If adverse conditions should begin.
The moment you need a guiding light
I will be there again.

Inspired by the value of simply being there for each other.

Live Out Loud

I love the calm that's found in silence
I love the calm before the storm.
I love the babbling of a flowing brook
And the crackling of a fire so warm.

I love the joy of my child's laughter
I love the sound of a kiss goodnight.
I love the little voice that calls me "Daddy."
And the small arms that hold me tight.

I love the symphony of nighttime creatures
I love the birds when the day is bright.
I love the sound of the pounding rain
That lulls me to sleep at night.

But most of all a simple "Thanks"
Or love whispered in my ear,
Have got to be the two best sounds
I most often like to hear.

Because the sound of gratitude
Most elevates my spirit.
And reminds me that my life has value
Every single time I hear it.

I love to live my life out loud
Not only through my ear.
I love the sounds that touch my spirit
Because that's the best way to hear.

*Inspired by the need we all have to be told that we've done
something right and that we're appreciated for who we are and
what we do.*

Just Then

When I awoke I opened my eyes
I stretched, I yawned and let out a sigh.
I sat up in bed so my day could begin.
I had nothing else to do just then.

I walked to the sink to brush my teeth.
Then showered scrubbing from head to feet.
I stood and enjoyed being clean again,
I had nothing else to do just then.

I ate my breakfast after a restful night.
And my hunger lessened with every bite.
I cleaned my plate and wiped my chin.
I had nothing else to do just then.

While driving I listened and looked around
Beyond speeding cars and honking sounds.
Enjoying the silence between the din.
I had nothing else to do just then.

At work I find joy from the great benefit
Of who I choose to be while doing it.
Enjoying the now that follows each then.
I had nothing else to do just then.

But soon another day has departed
I'm a little bit better than when I started.
I reflect upon the day that has been.
I had nothing else to do just then.

I work my work and live my day.
I live I love and grow along the way.
Then I lie my head down for sleep again.
I had nothing else to do just then.

Inspired by the value of living in the moment. I have found it the greatest way for managing stress by pacing myself and taking things one at a time. I've also found it to be the best way of making sure I give every moment of my life the attention it deserves.

Limitations

What do I know of my limits?
And what am I limited from?
Am I limited in what I can do
And thus in who I become?

What force determines what limits me?
Is it a fact of the human condition?
Am I surrounded by obstacles
Or only ego-induced supposition?

Is a limit imposed on me from without
By a person or society?
Are these limitations always true
Or only when I agree?

Are limitations only those
That are perceived as such?
Could it be that my perceptions
Are what limit me so much?

Am I truly hindered by such limitations
That I've learned to trust as so?
Or can I find true freedom
From letting these perceptions go?

It is often said that the sky is the limit
Of this notion I must beware.
For I may never know the joy of freedom
If I keep on stopping there.

Inspired by the fact that so many Aspies are limited as much if not more by their own self doubt than by any challenges presented by their unique neurology.

The Miracle Question

What if as you slept tonight
A miracle occurred?
I'd like you to consider this
It's not at all absurd.

Now imagine that when you awoke
You noticed something strange.
You're life is not as it was before
Because it completely changed.

Your life has become the kind of life
You'd always dreamed it could be.
But how do you know that something's different?
Is it by something that you see?

How do you know the miracle happened?
What is different from the day before?
Are there things that there are fewer of
While others there are more?

How has your life now improved
Since this miracle took place?
What do you detect as different
In sight and touch and taste?

Once you've listed all these changes
There is one thing left to do.
You must change them all from simple answers
And make them all come true.

Inspired by the fact that change in many instances takes as long as you decide it will. The decision that you make to change the direction of your life can be made this instant. What often prevents change from happening isn't because change is difficult. It's because your willingness to commit and follow through is difficult. Though I admit I have had difficulty following through on some of the harder choices. I was able to after realizing that allowing an unacceptable present to continue would be even harder to endure than change.

My Family

Today I honor my parents
Not just the parents of my birth.
I honor my Father in Heaven
And my precious Mother Earth.

Today I honor my family.
My sisters and my brothers.
The offspring of my Heavenly Father
And my generous Earthly Mother.

I honor every man and woman
Of every creed and every color.
For we share a sacred heritage
A seamless connection to each other.

Today my family reunion begins
When I return home each day
I've met many more of my brothers and sisters
And they met me today.

Our greatest gift to our family tree
Is to make our parents proud
By generously reaching out to each other
And serving each other somehow.

When we come together as family
We rise more often than we fall.
We do this for our parents and for each other
We are family after all.

Inspired by the belief that if we all saw and acted toward each other in this way, the spirit of family created by it could become the envy of the universe.

My Life Team

"Batter up" the umpire said
The game you see must go ahead.
But this is no routine contest
Where one team is trying to be the best.

This game is the one I live each day
While walking through life and making my way.
A life that is a series of plays
Where the outcome isn't always my way.

Sometimes I walk sometimes I run
Sometimes it's work and sometimes fun.
Each base a goal as I move about
Sometimes I'm safe sometimes I'm out.

Thank goodness I am not alone
But surrounded by others whose metal is shown
By what they bring to my life team
They support me while I live my dream.

Whenever an effort I decide to mount
I go to my Starters on whom I can count.
They are always faithful and by me they stand
They are first in line to lend a hand.

Next are my Sneezers who are filled with cheer
Their praise and encouragement fill my ear.
They are always there to believe in me
Only seeing the best I can be.

Also the Shovers appear in my way
They hope my progress to delay.
Their actions designed to make me fail
For when I lose they can prevail.

The Shouters also stand in my way
With all the negative things they say.
When to these words I choose to submit
Only then am I likely to quit.

When I a Shover and Shouter do meet
How can Starters and Sneezers hope to compete?
They do so when their numbers exceed
What negativity needs to succeed.

The more Starters and Sneezers I happen to know
The more likely that I am to grow.
My chances of living the life that I dream
Are only as good as those on my team.

Inspired by the fact that we rely upon the people and the things around us to make us better and find our way through life. Aspies need to understand that asking for help isn't a sign of weakness. It's a sign of intelligence that stems from knowing that we learn and grow by asking questions. I've learned that I'm able to accomplish so much more by asking for help when I realize that my current abilities are insufficient for the job so I ask to borrow the strengths of others. I don't know anyone who did anything to make the world better all by themselves. There is nothing to be gained by remaining ignorant when the information you need is there for the asking.

My Little Man

I still remember that special morning
When I heard your mother say
A new life was growing inside her womb
And that you were on the way.

I pressed my ear against her middle
And heard the beating of your heart.
Then as a tear rolled down my cheek
The beating of mine did start.

I watched you grow for all those months
And felt the swelling of my pride.
Because I knew the day was soon
When you'd be at my side.

But then the day had finally come
When I held you in my arms.
And I made you a solemn promise
That I'd keep you safe from harm.

For you are my beloved son
And I'll be the best Dad that I can.
I love my son with all my heart.
Because you're my little man.

Inspired by my boys, Zach, Aidan and Connor. My constant reminders that I am responsible for more than myself. That I am the one they look to to learn what the world is like and what the world has to offer them. It is also my responsibility to prepare them for the world. Equally as important, it is my responsibility to prepare the world to receive them.

My Wings Won't Fly

I was gliding through the sky one day.
When suddenly something got in my way.
For a moment there was no sight or sound.
Then I awoke lying motionless upon the ground.

I surely but slowly began to awake.
I tried moving my wings but the move wouldn't take.
I moved my feet and I opened each eye.
I felt a terrible pain and began to cry.

I looked at my wings each had a terrible break.
I tried to move them again but no move would they make.
I tried and I tried my heaven's how I tried.
But soon I knew that my wings wouldn't fly.

I walked for what seemed like eternity
Without my wings I no longer felt free.
What good is a bird without its wings?
When I could fly I could do so many things.

I was angry, and fearful, and sad for awhile.
But just the other day my face found a smile.
For as I walked and walked I did now feel
That my broken wings were beginning to heal.

I can move them a little bit more each day.
How long it will take I really can't say.
But I am determined one day to return to the sky.
So I'll do whatever it takes until my wings do fly.

Inspired by my dear friend Mary who is a walking miracle. A few years ago she was driving on a rainy day and her car was struck on the drivers side by a gravel truck that lost control on wet pavement. She survived multiple surgeries to repair two shattered femurs, a broken pelvis, a shattered arm, two collapsed lungs, broken ribs and other injuries I can't remember. I wrote this for her surprise 60th birthday party that we celebrated in the cafeteria of the rehabilitation hospital where she was learning to get back on her feet using legs now held together with metal plates and screws.

Mary is very special to me because from the moment I met her she always accepted me for who I am and never asked me to be anything more. Mary is the embodiment of the life lesson that success comes from getting back up every time you're knocked down. She survived through the miracle of modern medicine and the miracle of the attitude to keep on moving no matter how hard it is to do so. So when someone tells me something is hard to do, I tell them about Mary and they almost feel embarrassed for having the nerve to think their challenge was hard.

Mary is now enjoying an early retirement at home with her husband where she walks on her own without assistance, tending her garden and living her life. Her wings have healed and she flies once again. She keeps moving forward and she keeps getting up whenever she's down. She's one of my many heroes. Go get em Mary.

One Last Lullaby

There comes a time in every life
When we must say goodbye.
And now that time for me has come
For one last lullaby.

I sing the song of those I've loved
And who have loved me in return.
I smile at all of the memories
And of the lessons that I've learned.

I am filled with endless gratitude
For the lives I've been able to touch.
I shed a tear for those I love
Because I'll miss them all so much.

But now my body is starting to slow
And soon it will certainly die.
But the moment I take my final breath
My soul is set free to fly.

Until that time I will hold your hand
And ask that you hold mine.
My suffering will be over soon
When I enter into the divine.

My breath is getting softer now.
And my heart begins to slow.
So sing me one last lullaby
As I'm preparing to let go.

I close my eyes for one last time
As I enter eternal sleep.
I leave my body in this world
By my joys I get to keep.

I release the hand I hold in this life
And grab hold of another one.
Although I have left so much behind.
There is so much more to come.

As you look upon me now.
Without breath and without pulse.
Remember that my life has not ended.
I've just taken it somewhere else.

Inspired by my first job after graduate school which was as a Hospice Social Worker. I sat with many families as they watched a loved one peacefully take their last breath. I was inspired as I listened to patients and their families tell stories about lives. These families and patients taught me so much. I wrote this poem as an effort to support them during a difficult time. I let it also serve as a reminder that the journey toward my final breath is paved by the memories I create for other people and how I matter in their lives. I learned that people don't remember you for the things you have or even the things you did. What they remember is what the things you did meant to them.

On Purpose

To live your life on purpose
Is to chart a meaningful course.
You pursue your goals with focus
And a passion driven force.

Your purpose is for what you live
With strength you are endowed.
For when you have a powerful "why"
You have endurance for any "how."

The progress of humanity
Has been championed by the few
Who had a glorious sense of purpose
With which to guide them through.

A single, slender Indian man
Embraced poverty and ridicule.
Guided by his sense of purpose
Freed his country from foreign rule.

An unassuming Catholic Nun
Once her purpose was declared.
Opened her arms to a nation of poor
And took them all into her care.

An African-American man
Who discovered his life station
Led the fight for civil rights
Changing the course of an entire nation.

With purpose entire mountains move
Along with the course of civilization
That can either be used to build or destroy
A single or many nations.

Or purpose can simply be used by you
For your daily motivation.
But history shows the bigger the purpose
The greater the salvation.

Inspired by a few of my heroes, Gandhi, Mother Theresa and Martin Luther King Jr. Each of them saw an aspect of the human condition that they knew was unacceptable and needed to be addressed. Instead of passing the buck they took responsibility to get the change started. We are experiencing a similar situation now with the mistreatment of those on the Autism Spectrum. A cause I and many others have taken the responsibility to address. One thing in life is certain, if you don't stand for something there's no reason to get up.

The Power Of One

"Which one are you?"

Are you, or have you ever met the:
Athletic one
Best one
Brightest one
Creative one
Crazy one
Dependable one
Dumb one
Fat one
First one
Funny one
Great one
Happy one
Independent one
Jealous one
Last one
Loud one
Middle one
Next one
New one
Normal one

Number one
One everybody turns to
One nobody talks about
Old one
Other one
Pretty one
Respectable one
Responsible one
Quiet one
Reliable one
Right one
Skinny one
Short one
Smart one
Sweet one
Successful one
Shy one
Talented one
Tall one
Thin one
This one
That one
Weird one
Wrong one
Young one
Or are you simply
THE ONE AND ONLY?

Inspired by a tradition I began when my second son, Aidan, was born. My first born, Zach, was afraid he'd lose my love to his brother and flat out asked me if he was still my favorite. I explained to him that he would always be my number one Zach, and his brother would be my number one Aidan. That way each of my children would always know that the answer to the question "Which one are you?" will always be "I am the number one me."

Whichever one you determine yourself to be, you must remember one thing: Who you are or who you've come to think of yourself as is a mere shadow of who you can become. The one you are now is not the one you will be forever. Who you are now is simply the seed for the one you are meant to be. If you're going to be one, be one who learns, grows, and helps everyone become better ones. If anyone can do it, you're the one.

Practicing The Art Of You

To do anything with a degree of skill
You must practice every day.
If you get lazy with your regimen
Your proficiency will decay.

This fact is undeniable
For every skill it's true.
Nowhere else is it more important
Than when it comes to being you.

I've seen person after person
Who are the best at their profession.
Their practice never included themselves
Often leaving them in depression.

This is not to say that physical skill
Isn't important to have and know.
But when you neglect to practice yourself
You will lack the skills to grow.

As an artist practices with many a brush,
A dancer looks for the right shoes.
If you don't work to refine yourself
What you don't use you will lose.

As you set your daily schedule
With all the exercise you include,
Add some time to practice qualities
You aspire to exude.

If you want to be more patient
Or more loving to your spouse.
Then schedule time to practice it
When together in your house.

If you wish to be more focused
Or for your listening to improve.
Begin to make appointments
To make it part of your daily groove.

Practicing the art of being you
Is so often not included
In any academic teaching
It's no wonder we get deluded.

However important the other things are
That you practice to get ahead.
You'll go much further when you first practice
Inside your heart and in your head.

Inspired by the fact that people often concentrate on becoming the best at a career or at a certain skill. It is also about the fact that in school where students are encouraged to be the best in the class, to get the best grades. Never are they encouraged to be the best human being they can be. I would love to see a school curriculum that included how to be a decent human being. As it is, bullying, backstabbing and gossip are seen as parts of the school experience. Is it a wonder why our school system is so lacking and our special needs students are suffering when they are encouraged to learn social skills by interacting with those exhibiting a pattern of poor character that the school system sees fit to ignore.

Of course there are schools that rise to the occasion and address these issues. But they do so because they choose to on their own, not because it is seen as something that needs to be an essential part of the education of children. In my opinion the most rewarding accomplishment in life is becoming a quality human being. Why not encourage our children to compete for that accomplishment?

The Prince Of Perseverance

Here's a story about a man named Prince
Who was clumsy and full of doubt.
In spite of his efforts at fitting in
He was always counted out.

The men in his village each had a skill,
At which each was a master.
Prince had neither a job nor a skill.
Each day his dream faded faster.

Prince had a single lasting dream,
Although everyone called it dumb.
It was, he hoped, that maybe one day,
A Knight he would become.

Deep down inside he felt that he
Would never have the chance
To sit proudly on a horse's back
Wearing armor and holding a lance.

Then one day outside the castle
He heard the Town Crier declare,
"A phenomenal event was about to take place,
And the King would like all to be there."

He said, "For the first time
The King would invite
The chance for every willing man
To contest to be a Knight."

Prince was the first in line,
His dream now close in sight.
He didn't consider that in order to win
He must combat a Knight.

The Knight that he was scheduled to joust
Was incredibly strong and skilled.
But Prince decided to take the chance,
The chance of being killed.

So Prince would practice every day
Along the jousting course.
He would lose his balance while holding his lance
And kept falling off his horse.

He tried and tried to keep his balance
But he really needed help.
So he sought the aid of a jousting master
Whose name was Mr. Phelps.

Prince practiced all that he was taught
But Phelps would only frown.
Prince's arms were very weak
So his lance dragged on the ground.

It was now two days before the joust
And Prince's chances stunk.
Phelps just gave up hope and said,
"You're on your own good luck."

Soon the people filled the streets
The day of the joust had arrived.
If Prince still hoped to be a Knight
The joust he must survive.

He felt his chances weren't that good,
His hopes of winning faded.
He began to fear he'd only fail
And leave humiliated.

His inner voice told him not to fight,
To find a way out somehow.
But this was his dream and he'd come this far
So he wouldn't give up now.

He grabbed his lance
And climbed on his horse.
He lost his balance
And fell off of course.

With a bruise on his pride he stood back up
Then tried to get back on his horse.
A shout was heard, "The joust is over."
Prince quickly discovered the source.

He saw a Knight, his opponent who said,
"I forfeit the fight.
I foolishly left my horse out
And he ran away last night."

This meant that Prince had won the joust,
By forfeit fair and square.
The King walked out to where he stood
And Knighted him right there.

"I'll never ask you to fight," He said
"All I ask is my men pay you homage.
When all was against you you persevered.
I am Knighting you for your courage."

He was Knighted Sir Prince of Perseverance
And the crowd let out a scream.
They kneeled to him then all bowed down
To show him their esteem.

He taught everyone a lesson that day,
To never throw your dreams away.
And it doesn't matter how hard things seem,
If you never give up, your will win your dream.

Though a fictional story it is inspired by the idea of a character who was physically clumsy in spite of his best efforts. While others gave up on him he never gave up on himself. He never let the word "can't" enter his mind. Though he achieved his dream in an unconventional way, it proved that perseverance pays off. It took me 12 years to complete 6 years of college. So what, I kept at it and look at me know. I wrote a book that you're holding in your hands and hopefully enjoying.

Problem vs. Challenge

What do you see the difference to be
Between a problem and a challenge?
The former is an obstacle
The latter you can manage.

This is not a simple play on words
Comparing two fruits from a common tree.
It is instead a mental shift.
That will alter what you see.

When you say, "I have a problem."
It means there's something wrong.
When you say, "I have a challenge."
Facing it makes you strong.

I've met a lot of people
Who face their problems with fear.
But when faced with a challenge
An opportunity appears.

You see the problem with a problem
Is that it's often viewed so badly.
While a challenge is the opposite
A gift you can accept so gladly.

If this idea is hard to grasp
Then let me take you by the hand.
I will show you an example
That will help you understand.

If you see a mountain as in your way
It's a problem that holds you back.
If you see a mountain that you can climb
Then you need some equipment to pack.

Remember life only presents with challenges
Because you can see anything through
There is nothing that can hold you back
There is no problem bigger than you.

Inspired by the fact that so many Aspies I meet shut down in the presence of anything difficult or frustrating in any way. Primarily because they perceive the discomfort of frustration as dangerous. Calling something a problem can make it appear as something that opposes or is against you. While a challenge is something provided for you to make you better. Problems deny you something, Challenges offer opportunities. This is your classic half empty half full predicament. If you're going to choose how to see something. You might as well choose a perspective that is useful.

The Quit Monster

This is a story about a monster
But not the one under my bed.
It's not the one inside my closet,
It's the one inside my head.

He's the one that always scares me
Every time I chase my dream.
At the moment I get going
He will take out all my steam.

The monster whispers in my ear
"Who do you think you are?
You're no good; you'll never make it
You'll never go that far."

But worst of all is when I listen
And let the monster's message in.
Then all I learn is how to quit
And never how to win.

But one day it suddenly came to me
I finally figured it out.
The monster always followed me
Because he fed upon my doubt.

Another thing I realized
Much later on that day
Was the monster had an allergy
That would make him run away.

So I dug down deep inside myself
And what I found within
Was a great big ball of confidence
That really got under his skin.

The more that I refused to quit
The more the monster would sob.
And soon I saw my dreams come true,
Once the quit monster was out of a job.

This one speaks for itself.

Reflections

I look into the mirror that is hung upon my wall
And whether I look good or bad it doesn't care at all.
It doesn't play the critic to what I choose to wear
It only shows the reflection of exactly what is there.

The mirror does not alter the images it reflects
It accepts things as they are and never does reject.
It does not cling to the images of any passerby.
It does not interfere at all but lets them pass right by.

When river waters are calmed all distortions disappear
Without any agitation my reflection is perfectly clear.
Only when the water is quieted without a ripple or a glare
Can the clarity of calmness show only what is there.

Water becomes distorted when into it something is tossed
And its original calmness is temporarily lost.
But when the object has settled the distortion is withdrawn.
It does not persist its agitation once the agitator is gone.

A polished window reflection is as clear and clean as light
Its reflective clarity is altered when dirt begins to alight.
If an unfettered reality is something you want to view
A well-polished window is what you must be looking through.

If my mind becomes a mirror, and I cling not to any image
I will be able to let things go with no judgmental damage.
If my mind is like the water that lets agitation pass
Then I have found the source of an inner peace that lasts.

If my mental window is continually polished
Delusion can be completely abolished.
With no blemish of dirt in my way
Every day is a very good day.

Inspired by the spirit of non-judgement and for accepting and respecting people and things for who they are. I admit I have given people the benefit of the doubt many times only to have them do me wrong. But the fault isn't mine for trusting them, the fault is theirs for abusing my trust.

The Sail Of Adversity

I gaze upon the boat as it begins
To push against the waters and the winds.
Its motor pushes hard to no avail.
The push of Mother Nature stands to prevail.

As the progress of the vessel begins to trail
The captain orders the crew to raise the sail.
With a gust of wind the sail is full and strong.
Now the boat begins to swiftly move along.

The secret is when adversity starts to win
That you must act to take the lead again.
When any kind of force begins to push you
The opposite of its efforts is what you do.

You pull so that you can remain stable.
Thus the adversity is unbalanced and disabled.
No matter if the strength of the force is stronger
When you utilize it it commands no longer.

An obstacle or barrier is only such
If you allow it to stand in your way too much.
Adversity's relationship to you
Depends strictly on your point of view.

One secret to success in life
Is learning to make an ally of strife.
Instead of it causing you to hesitate
Let it be a catalyst to motivate.

Whenever you experience resistance
Use its energy to your assistance.
But make sure no matter what you do
That you are in front, and it's not in front of you.

Inspired by the spirit of cooperation with change instead competing against or resisting it. The fact of that matter is that all movement in life occurs one of two ways, either by pushing or pulling.

When we walk, our feet and legs push us in the direction we want to go. A sailboat moves when the wind pulls the sails, making the boat move in the direction it wants to go. A baby is born through a combination of pushing and pulling. Adversity occurs when we concentrate our efforts on fighting the direction things are going instead of moving with them. The principle "When pushed pull, when pulled push" is a guiding principles of some of the most powerful martial arts systems ever devised. The lesson is simple: When you encounter resistance or adversity of any kind, the way to turn it from an adversary into an ally is by utilizing its energy instead of resisting it. If you're feeling pushed in life, don't push back; pull instead. And when pulled against your will, push. In this way you can maintain your balance in life because you are doing what is required to stay balanced instead of exhausting yourself in your efforts to resist adversity.

Some of the best examples of this principle are found in recreational sports. Did anyone ever see the point in taking a piece of wood and running into the ocean to actively try to stop a wave from coming in? Of course not, that would be ridiculous. But it did occur to someone to climb on that piece of wood and cooperate with the power of the incoming wave, hence, the invention of surfing. By working with the natural direction of the wave and allowing it to push you while standing on a properly designed board, a natural force that could have been an adversity has suddenly become an ally once you discover how to approach it and do so with the right tool or attitude. I guess the lesson here is in order for adversity to propel you forward, you must stand in front of it instead of letting it stand in front of you.

Two of the greatest pullers of our era were Mahatma Gandhi and Dr. Martin Luther King, Jr. When the forces of ignorance, fear, and cruelty at the hands of their oppressors pushed them, they patiently and with unwavering tenacity worked to pull their oppressors into an understanding. This understanding led to an increased freedom to be enjoyed by millions of people. However, after each of those great men was assassinated, many of their followers regressed to pushing back, and much of what pulling had accomplished was lost. Those on the autism spectrum are in a similar situation today as we are confronted by those who are pushing for a "cure" or pushing us to be just like them. When I say "cure" I'm referring to those who negate the positives in those on the spectrum and only see it for the challenges. I'm not arguing against the often valuable methods for addressing other health issues such as digestive issues which cause physical pain. I happen to experience horrendous digestive problems from ingesting dairy products. It is possible to address these issues while respecting the individual. Unfortunately there are those who don't separate the two. There are those that believe there is a neurotypical person trapped inside an autistic brain.

It is my hope that we can pull this thinking into an understanding of the value Aspies provide society by being who we are in spite of their perspective that is only often able to see who we aren't. Remember, when pushed, pull; when pulled, push.

School of Life

I was almost late for class today
But it doesn't really matter.
The lesson would find me anyway
For life is my educator.

It doesn't matter what the grade
Or even what the class
It only matters of what I'm made
That determines whether I pass.

From moment to moment you'll never know
What lessons life is arranging
Class is never boring or slow
Because the lesson plan keeps changing.

Each and every single day
Life will offer you a test
To see if down you'll choose to lay
Or stand and give your best.

The lessons that will help you grow
Are never learned with ease.
Wisdom you will never know
By only getting what you please.

The more life classes that you pass
The more that you will learn.
Knowing that the wisdom amassed
Was yours alone to earn.

Inspired by the unique journey we each walk through life in which every moment of every day gives you a chance to slow, grow or stay the same. It is up to you and you alone in which direction you choose to move, backward, forward or nowhere at all.

Sowing The Seed

I sigh and let my eyes cast down.
I fix them upon the fractured ground.
I observe the soil all dried from drought.
It is pale and riddled with cracks throughout.

It opens wide to the coming rain,
Its thirst is quenched till no cracks remain.
Opening up does not make it weak.
It makes it in need and willing to seek.

This is a strength and not vulnerability.
Allows itself the help for vitality.
The soil regains its strength and fertility.
Allowing an opening for strengthened integrity.

The tree above begins to shed it seeds.
The soil below is exactly what they need.
The soil lets seeds in and the next thing you know
Where a seed was planted new life now grows.

I know now what appears as inadequacy,
When I experience vulnerability,
Is an opening, in which life can begin,
When I let the seeds of growth come in.

I look now at the soil of my being.
There are an endless number of openings I'm seeing.
If I eventually let all vulnerability out,
There is an endless amount of new growth that can sprout.

Inspired by the fear of vulnerability that many Aspies have. I hear them talk about appearing weak, stupid or like they can't do something. My response to them is if there are things they aren't good at or things they don't know do they honestly think that by keeping to themselves that people won't notice.

I further add that not knowing and choosing to remain ignorant by not admitting to it so you can learn is a greater sign of weakness than admitting it having the courage to ask for information and growing.

The fact of the matter is that if you don't know something you only don't know it once. Meaning that the moment you ask for and get the information you will never not know it again. Therefore forget about not wanting to appear vulnerable and instead think about how to appear teachable. People who are ready to learn and grown spend a lot less time being afraid and frustrated over not knowing something because they're eagerly in the pursuit of knowing more. The people who make the greatest difference in life aren't the know it alls, it's the learn it alls.

Still Aspie After All These Years

I look upon my sorted past
A confusing world that seemed so vast.
I struggled as I made my way.
So hard to get started every day.

So often it would be too much
The world seemed so out of touch.
When I could simply take no more
I'd completely melt and the tears would pour.

They would try to help but didn't know how.
Wish I knew then what I know now.
I'd tell them I did the best I could
If I could've done better you know I would.

As the years went on I found a way
To fake fitting in and myself betray.
As long as the critics were satisfied
I'd avoid being socially crucified.

Now so many years have past
I'm free to be myself at last.
The Aspie within is going strong
Though I'm well equipped to get along.

Though I'm able to make fewer social mistakes
Tremendous effort it always takes.
Don't be fooled by how normal things appear
I'm still Aspie after all these years.

Inspired by years of not knowing I was an Aspie and going through hell without support as a result. It's also to point out that although I've managed to master enough social conventions to sometimes avoid detection, it is accomplished with tremendous effort and often leads to exhaustion.

Sometimes I think I'm doing myself an extreme disservice as people either doubt I'm an Aspie or are so used to my convincing facade that they are intolerant when I'm too tired to keep it up. One day I hope I can be as aspie as I want to be and the world won't give it a second thought.

The Stop Sign

The soldier with the crimson face
Stands erect and deeply rooted in place.

He diligently waits for all who approach
His commitment to safety beyond reproach.

He expresses but a single word.
That need only be seen and never heard.

Those who take heed and his warning abide
Will spare a moment to pause at his side.

Then proceed beyond the paths intersect,
Saved by the soldier who quietly protects.

*Inspired by my desire to see things as more than they seem in
the spirit of always trying to see the best in everything. I wrote
this while looking at a stop sign and trying to see it less as an
object and more as something possessing character. If I can see
such greatness in a stop sign, imagine what you can find in your-
self with the goal of seeing more than you're seeing now.*

The Student

Every day the sun rises refreshed.
And every day for me is a test.
Of how good a student that day I can be.
Shall I rise to the top or fail miserably.

If I wish to learn all that is taught this day
I must remember to proceed in a certain way.
My mind must be open to receive
Not to project as I presumptuously conceive.

My mind always aware that all I have learned
Is subject to change at every turn.
For the moment I establish a rule in my mind
An exception can be found causing the rule to unwind.

Old age is not a guarantee that we have become more prudent.
It only means we've had opportunities to become a better student.
My life will not revolve around the acquisition of rigid knowledge.
Instead every waking moment will be my first day at college.

For the moment I think I know something to be true.
Is the moment I forget the student's cardinal rule
That change is the only rule in life that applies.
In this rule is where a lifelong, open-minded student lies.

I shall be the eternal beginner without a prejudice in sight.
I will never be arrogant or look always to be right.
My ideas will not define me so I can be open at every turn.
I will only be a student who is ready and eager to learn.

Inspired by the fact that it's more valuable to always be curious than always be right. I've met too many people who allow their expertise to get in the way of their learning. As they believe they're equipped with immaculate perception, any conversation with them becomes a battle of facts instead of an exploration for learning. I've found that one of the true joys of living is found in the sharing of meaning and experiences.

No matter how well you feel you know something, remember that the only thing you've mastered is your own understanding and you have an endless supply of teachers as you share your meaning with others. Then, as a humble student, seek to learn from their meanings.

One thing I suggest to further this perspective is to make a point of learning at least one new thing everyday. Whether it is learning a new word or meeting a new person, eating something or somewhere new for lunch. Anything that allows you to experience something new keeps you fresh. It also puts you in a place where any opportunity that you may not have experienced otherwise may occur.

For example, I met my wife on the first day of a new job that I had originally turned down a week earlier. But when I discovered the job I'd chosen wouldn't provide enough opportunity for growth, I went back and was hired. Had my attitude not been to put myself in situations where I knew learning could take place, we would not have met.

Supposed To

Do I do what I'm supposed to do,
When I do things overall?
When I look at it are there things
That I'm supposed to do at all?

I wonder what would happen
If I never really knew,
What the things in life there are
That I'm supposed to do?

What if I
Were just to decide
That all "supposed to's"
Are merely contrived?

I guess one thing
That I could do,
Is for once in my life
To do something new.

One thing that
May happen then,
The rigid "supposed to's"
May have to bend.

I may be allowed
To be more myself.
A possible step
Toward much better health.

Now I have one final question
That I'd like to ask of you:
What might occur if you never do other
Than the things you are supposed to?

Inspired by those who spend a lot of time denying who they are in favor of trying to be "normal" because they've gotten the impression that they will only be loved when they are like everyone else. Here's the problem. In the useless pursuit of trying not to be different you somehow miss that everyone is different but they're trying so hard to be the same.

The reason why no one succeeds at being normal is because it's a goal that cannot be accomplished in a world where everyone is designed to be unique. Somewhere someone who didn't like himself thought he'd be happier if he were someone else and set a rotten example by trying to do so. I can't remember the last time someone succeeded in life because he was the best at being normal. Those who succeed are the ones who realize and accept that the way things are supposed to be done only result in keeping the things the way they've always been. By embracing what makes you different, allows you to do different, and the world becomes different as a result of interacting with you. If you want the world and it's progress to come to a screeching halt then by all means do what you're supposed to, strive to be everything you're not. Then while you're holding yourself back, those who are willing to be themselves will be busy changing the world for the better.

Thanks For Being You

As a child I was often asked
"What is wrong with you?"
This question caused me so much pain
It was a question about my value.

Why would people ask such things?
What a terrible thing to say
To an innocent and curious child
Who's simply trying to find his way.

Why is different also bad?
That's the message I would get.
If I ever felt good about myself
That's a feeling I'd soon forget.

Just because someone is unique
Doesn't make what they do wrong.
It isn't bad to make you question
What you've been doing all along.

You'd think you'd want a child to know
They're a worthy human being.
Not only when you approve of them
Or like what you are seeing.

Any child who walks through life
Is a student this is a true.
But if you're open to the lesson
The child can teach you too.

There's a unique opportunity
When a special child is born
It's an opportunity to grow
Not to feel bad and mourn.

A special child who works so hard
For what you find easy to do.
Gives you the chance to help this child
And become a better you.

The help this child needs the most
Isn't to be normal at any cost.
By working hard for sameness
What matters most is often lost.

It's easy to miss the value in something
When all you notice is what's missing.
When all you see are challenges
Make sure the strengths you aren't dismissing.

Instead of working so very hard
For the child you think you are due.
Why not become the type of parent
Your special child can use?

This world has had enough of normal
And look what it's become.
Perhaps it's time for a little change
So look out here we come.

Life is a complex puzzle
Where only different pieces fit.
In a puzzle the different pieces are normal
And of the greatest benefit.

We are at a special turning point
In the course of human events.
When what it means to be a person
We can actively reinvent.

There is a place for all of us
To be exactly who we are.
And do the best with what we've got
Together we'll go so far.

Some day you'll be able to look at me
And others with differences to.
And instead of asking what is wrong
You'll say "Thanks for being you."

Inspired by all the horrible comments made to and about people on the spectrum each and every day under the guise of being helpful. All the correction and criticism that does more to tear a person down when you're mission ought to be to lift them up. Thank goodness that through the seas of people seemingly lining up to tell me everything I was doing wrong, there were the special few who believed in me. I am blessed to be who I am today because of those who told me, I can do, I am worth it and that what's different about me is what's right about me.

Three Pillars of Success

Know myself is first in line
One of three pillars intertwined.
When who I am I can define
Success occurs to my design.

When I learn what makes me tick
My path through life is mine to pick.
To live my strengths is the real trick
To live my challenges will make me sick.

Respect myself is pillar two
I accept my strengths and challenges too.
I am kind in all I say and do
When referring to my own value.

I believe my life will always count
To something special my efforts amount.
For all my successes I can account
Any adversity I can surmount.

Self Advocate is number three
When mistreatment is done to me.
I educate so others can see
Accepting is what they need to be.

I let it be known when I'm in need
When to keep your distance and when to proceed.
In living my life I take the lead
To see to it that I succeed.

For when I know I make the grade
With a confidence that doesn't fade
A life worth living is my crusade
To show the world of what I'm made.

Inspired by my Three Pillars for Success with Asperger's, 1) Self Awareness, 2) Self Respect, 3) Self Advocacy. Unless you know who you are you won't know your strengths and challenges. Unless you respect who you are for your strengths and challenges you won't do right by yourself. Unless you step up and use your strengths you won't move forward in life. Unless you speak up for yourself others cannot guide and support you as you travel on your way through the life you're meant to live.

The Time

Do you happen to know the time right now?
If you're unable to tell I will show you how.
Those who can really tell time are truly rare
But I will teach you how without a moment to spare.

Let's begin with the magical moment of birth,
When did you begin this life on Earth?
Now think of your greatest joy to date
How long did it last by the ticking clock's rate?

Now imagine a moment from a time to come,
A glimpse into the you that you hope to become.
How far off does that future lie?
What length of time would you specify?

Well no matter what moment you choose to name
Whether past or future they are one in the same.
For to live in the moment is easily done
Because since the beginning there has only been one.

The illusion of linear time we've created
Needs to be officially negated.
The new perception I offer in exchange
Is one moment in a state of perpetual change.

Inspired by my perception that time is but a single moment in a state of perpetual change. It is my belief that there is no past, present or future. There is only this moment that keeps readjusting itself due to everything in it that keeps interacting with each other in new ways. Think of it as a piece of clay that you keep forming in different shapes. Same clay, different shape. I know this idea will be lost on the majority of people. It came about by my Aspergian tendency to live in the present. As you can imagine it's difficult to live in the present and be ambitious simultaneously. Therefore I thought of a way I could live in the present but be constantly observing the dance of change in the moment. That way I could be always aware of where I'm at as well as where I'm going. Think about this for a while and hopefully it will eventually have some use for you.

Two Steps

I took two steps in life today
In the direction I wish to move
Two more steps than yesterday
So that I might improve.

Make sure that I learn something new
Is the first step that I take.
So before this day is through
A new discovery I will make.

I share the lesson I have learned
And the second step is done.
At first a student and then in turn
A teacher I become.

I place one foot in front of the other
Toward a better life you see.
I help myself and then another
On the way to a better me.

*Inspired by my Two Goals for Everyday Life, 1) Learn Something
2) Teach Something. By learning something new each day you
guarantee yourself that life will never become routine, redundant*

and boring. You will always be curious, learning and growing. When you share what you've learned it can be the foundation of starting a conversation or simply passing on some helpful information. Ideally when you teach something you help someone else learn something and perhaps their day will be better in some way because you took the time to share.

Victory Lap

Today I make myself a promise
This pledge I now recite.
To keep a written record
Of everything that I do right.

I will celebrate my successes
No matter great or small.
Each one reflects my competence
So I celebrate them all.

No longer will I allow little things
To trouble me all day long.
I'll allow the wave of victory
To carry me along.

Whenever I get up on time
I'll give acknowledgment.
For I celebrate every single time
I show I am consistent.

My successes greatly increase in number
When this habit is utilized.
All the credit I'd forgotten to give myself
Is now being emphasized.

As time goes on I keep my list
And what will inevitably be found
Is that I begin to walk a victory lap
Each time my foot hits the ground.

Inspired by the value of every success, no matter how small. As the above lesson suggests, a powerful change of perception can occur when you begin to keep a written record of every success you experience. Even when you trip and fall, if you succeed in getting back up, that is a success. When you get to an appointment on time, give yourself credit. Write it down. When you begin to note what you do well, you will also begin to take note of what you did to achieve that success, therefore, increasing the likelihood that it will be repeated.

I know far too many people who consider themselves failures not because they don't succeed because in their mind the only successes that matter are the big ones. They've clearly missed that big successes are the culmination of little successes along the way.

By focusing on what you didn't get you give all of your energy to an attitude of failure. It is when you punish yourself for your imperfections and give those habits your undivided attention that you train your mind to remember how to take those steps again. Some people wonder why mistakes are repeated when they spend so much time memorizing how to do it.

Earl Nightingale once said, "We become what we think about, all day long." Are you getting the point? Focus your mind on your successes; remind yourself how to repeat those steps and you will. Success isn't a matter of luck, it's a matter of habit.

If you want to change the direction your life is going you must first change the direction your mind is going. Keep a diary of your successes. After all, a diary is a written record of your life. Imagine all of the parts you've been missing until now.

Whatever It Takes

If I wish to see my dreams take flight
I must make sure my mind is right.
Before I take a single step
My attitude I have to prep.

If my intention is simply to try
Then I can kiss my dreams goodbye.
For I am likely to hesitate
Success I will not celebrate.

If I decide to do my best
Still I may not pass the test.
For when the going gets too tough
My best may not be good enough.

There is one way for me to proceed
If success is to be guaranteed.
I commit to do whatever it takes
Because there is so much at stake.

I want my life to be truly great
So I cannot afford to hesitate.
I will always see things through
By doing whatever I need to do.

Inspired by the motivation to never give up.

When I Stood Up

There was a time when I sat still
Feeling powerless to act.
I was too afraid to make a move
My only option to react.

I focused on the sadness of life
Hope was so hard to see.
Never noticing joy was mine to create
Assuming life simply happened to me.

That changed the day when I stood up
More empowered than before.
I act to create a better life
To be a victim never more.

Inspired by those I've met who choose to be recipients of life instead of creators of life. So many for whatever reason perceive themselves as someone life happens to. They decide to react to life instead of being proactive and take the steps to create the life they want.

Where The Sun Don't Shine

There is an epidemic condition
Sometimes tricky to detect.
It can occur in any person
Even while standing quite erect.

The effect of this condition
Renders a person mentally blind.
The cause is having one's head stuck
In a place the sun don't shine.

Oh my, what a dreadful condition.
Isn't there something we can do?
So far a cure has been difficult
Cause it's a condition that we choose.

There are people who avoid the truth
Or deny what causes them worry.
To avoid confronting these concerns
Shove their heads in that place in a hurry.

These people are also often lacking
In basic common sense.
Avoiding opportunities to acquire it
At their own and others expense.

They ignore the consequences
That their actions do produce.
And never learn the methods
To help these outcomes to reduce.

Instead they keep their poor head stuck
In a place the sun don't shine.
Instead of creating solutions
They just stand around and whine.

*Inspired by those who walk around life with a self-inflicted con-
dition I call it C.R.I.S., which stands for Cranial-Rectal Insertion
Syndrome. This is the condition characterized by having your
head up your butt. The lesson you just read highlighted some of
the symptoms. These are people who ignore the law of cause
and effect. They are either surprised that their behavior has con-
sequences or simply choose to ignore those consequences. Their
C.R.I.S. is often seen to manifest in addition to Common Sense
Deficit Disorder. If you know people like this, do your utmost to
avoid them completely or at least minimize contact. It is epidem-
ic in my family and in many others. One of the more elusive
symptoms of C.R.I.S. is a deficiency in the sense of smell that
leaves them with the impression that their own feces is without
odor. The psychological ramifications of this smelling deficiency
leaves them believing that they're superior to others.*

*If you happen to see any of these symptoms in yourself, take
immediate steps to get your hands on an industrial strength
crowbar and a bottle of top-of-the-line shampoo. Then proceed
to pry your head loose from the place the sun don't shine. After
thoroughly washing your hair three or four times, begin taking
100 percent responsibility for your actions and the conse-
quences they create in your life and the lives of others. If you fail
to do so, you will likely see people avoiding your company or
you will see an epidemic of frustration in the people in your pres-
ence. It's your move.*

You also need to take an inventory of those people in your life who are toxic and those who are treasures. The toxic people are those who wear you down, seem to offer constant negativity at discount prices, and basically suck the energy from the room the moment they enter it. The treasures are those who bring you up, and contribute to the pleasant, nurturing moments of your life.

Once you've completed your list you may be surprised that people may appear on either list that you hadn't realized were such a burden or a blessing. This simple awareness is usually the key to beginning to minimize time with toxic people and maximize it with the treasures in your life. With this in mind, happy treasure hunting!

Wishing Upon A Star

When you wish upon a star
Don't plan on getting very far.
For if anything does come to you
It's because you decided to pursue.

Nothing much will ever come
When all you do is wish.
Action will always be required
For a goal you want to accomplish.

The sky is filled with endless millions
Of unanswered hopes and dreams.
Because they were released into the heavens
Instead of personally redeemed.

Some use a star for faithful guidance
When navigating the open sea.
But no star can complete the journey for you.
That responsibility lies with thee.

The power inside the greatest star
Is but a small and meager fraction.
When compared with the power that you release
When you back your dreams with action.

Inspired by those who wish for things to be given to them instead of taking the steps to work toward them.

The Worth Of Living

Is my life worth living?
If this life is even mine,
Does my life have a meaning?
Is there a reason I can find?

Do I play some grand significance
As the universe unwinds?
Or is life but an instant
A flickering light in the sky?

If worth lives only in my acquisitions
Then with them all worth wears out.
If worth lies in the fact that I am living.
Then worth lies endlessly throughout.

At this moment I ask myself
What am I living for?
Am I living for myself
Or living for others more?

Is being alive the greatest gift?
Or is its value something I ignore?
Through the empty worth of material things
I am always left wanting more.

Have I forgotten that life itself
Is by far the ultimate prize?
And through the simple joy of being alive
Can endless worth arise?

If still uncertain about the worth of life
And if I should decide to stay,
I will focus on the benefits of life,
That compelled me to stay today.

Inspired by the eternal question in search of the meaning of life. It is my contention that the meaning of life can be found in determining the place where your passion and ability meet. Every person is born enabled by his or her unique composite of biological magnificence with the ability to do at least one thing extremely well. However, this one thing usually only becomes apparent when the demands of our environment provides for its unveiling. Unfortunately many Aspies go through life with an upbringing that is filled with criticism and types of "can't programming" leaving them ill-equipped to explore their potential.

However, on some level I believe that every living thing is compelled in some way to do what it is designed to do best. Plants are compelled by design to produce oxygen and some a beautiful fragrance as well. Animals are compelled by their instincts to do what they're best at in order to play their unique part in the circle of life. As human beings I believe our passion and the ability to realize that passion compel us to do what we are each designed for.

What is passion? It is the focused drive that gets a person out of a burning house. The sheer determination that compels an athlete to ignore pain until a goal is achieved. Passion is the desire for something that is so strong you feel like you couldn't live without it. For some it is writing, painting, acting, playing a sport, etc. The one thing that gives their life more meaning than anything else that they can't live without is their passion. For me it is being of service to other Aspies in order to help them discover and maximize their own greatness. If I am not being of service I might as well not be living. What is it that you are as compelled to do, as you are to continue breathing, but also have the ability to do? For me it's writing poetry and public speaking. I thrive on communicating in any way possible. I give to others, and they give to me. I not only enjoy it--I also do this quite well. My passion and ability meet.

Some people struggle to define the purpose of their lives. I've learned firsthand that there is nothing that gets you out of bed in the morning faster and with greater vitality than a sense of purpose for your day and for your life. I walk through my day everyday with focus, clarity and an added bounce in my step while I watch others walk around tired, aimless and depressed. The only difference between me and them is that I know precisely what I'm doing it all for. So, what is the point of it all? Why bother getting up in the morning? There is only one answer to all of these questions, and the answer is "Whatever you want."

Wrapping The Diamond

Observe this very precious gem.
Just view this beautiful stone.
Comparable only to itself,
With a special value all its own.

Behold this simple diamond,
Which cannot be compromised.
It will always simply be itself
And never otherwise.

This diamond cannot be scratched or cracked
Or harmed in anyway.
With an indomitable integrity
A diamond it will always remain.

If I ever tried to color it
With brown, black, or blue.
It could only serve as decoration
For it remains a diamond through and through.

If it were wrapped in expensive packaging
That was most pleasing to my eye
Or even with simple and crumpled paper,
It is still a diamond wrapped inside.

If I placed it inside a short container,
Or a box that's six feet tall,
If I dropped it in a box ten feet wide,
Or in the thinnest box of all.

It wouldn't matter for a single moment
For the wrapping can never tell,
That behind all the external glitz,
There's a diamond in this shell.

The diamond is not its package.
Its value is not packaging defined.
No matter color, size, or shape,
The value is always found inside.

How true this is for the diamond
And for myself when I learn to see
The precious gem that gives me value
Is the diamond that is me.

Inspired by the power of the label and the help or harm that comes with it. The label Asperger's can be seen as a covering that obscures the value of the person behind the label. That is only true when you allow others to define what Asperger's mean as it pertains to you. No person is one dimensional with challenges alone, so allowing yourself to be defined in such a way is absurd. It is important that the wrapping you find yourself in reflects everything about you, your strengths and challenges alike. That way when someone sees what you're wrapped in they're excited to see what's inside. If you decide to use a term such as Asperger's to help define yourself, make sure the way you define it begins with everything that's right about you.

Thank You

Today I wrote a letter
Because the timing seemed just right.
I wrote a letter to myself
About all that I've done right.

It's time I broke the habit
Of focusing on all that I do wrong
When I really need to celebrate
All the things that make me strong.

I thank myself for all the times
I stuck with it in order to win.
Because I just believed in myself
When others thought I would give in.

I thank myself for who I am
And all that makes me worthy.
Whether others will treat me accordingly
Of this I no longer worry.

I thank myself for all I've learned
When the truth was hard to take.
I learn far less when things go right
And more when I make a mistake.

I thank myself for all my choices
Even those that cause me pain.
I thank me for taking responsibility
Instead of placing blame.

Finally I'll thank myself
From the bottom of my heart.
When I leave this world a better place
Than I found it at the start.

Inspired by the importance of being grateful to and for yourself even when others seem to let your positive efforts go unnoticed. In other words, catch yourself doing good and thank yourself for a job well done. You can even take it a step further and write yourself a thank you letter. Thank yourself for everything you're proud of, and clearly spell out how much you appreciate yourself.

Too often we go through life without the recognition we crave and deserve from others. Even worse is going without the recognition we deserve from ourselves. For this reason I suggest starting a new habit of writing yourself a thank you letter every now and then to show appreciation for yourself. You can even write a thank you letter to others for appreciating you. I think you'll find this will guarantee that you will experience a constant stream of gratitude even if you're only noticing it for yourself.

I've always enjoyed getting thank you letters because they let me know that I matter and that what I'm doing is of value. Just because others fail to notice at times and aren't grateful, doesn't mean I still don't deserve a thank you letter. So I write it myself. From this moment on when you need a little appreciation or just want to remind yourself that you are extremely valuable to yourself and the world, write yourself a letter. Then make sure you sign it:

With all my love and respect,

(Your Name)
P.S. I Love You

Yes, But!

Confidence can often shatter
The door to opportunity shut.
By treating success like it doesn't matter
In favor of a giant but.

This but is rooted in the mind
Where frustration is commonplace.
And accomplishments become hard to find
Even when staring you in the face.

It's easy to dismiss your gifts
With challenges so abundant.
Your journey toward self-doubt is swift
With thinking so redundant.

There is a way to turn things around
And keep the negative at bay.
The solution needed is simply found
By using your but a different way.

While now when strength is recognized
The compliment you quell.
The statement used to minimize
"But I have weaknesses as well."

What if you did the reverse instead
When someone offered you praise.
And turned the yes but on it's head.
By uttering the following phrase.

"Thank you for seeing what I do best
My efforts have shown through.
There are many challenges that I face
But I have many abilities too."

You see how easy it can be
To turn your thinking around.
When the positive you choose to see
A new outlook can be found.

Inspired by all the Aspies I've encountered that are so quick to minimize any mention of their strengths in favor of emphasizing their challenges. Deciding to see yourself through such negative eyes is like watering the weeds in your garden instead of the flowers. Do yourself the honor of weeding the garden of your mind and enjoying the flowers for once. You'll find that flowers grow much better when they're given some attention.

Afterward

This has been a mere sampling of the life lessons I've had the privilege to learn. If you would like, I will continue to share them as I encounter them. I would like to know if this book was useful to you. Please let me know by visiting my Web site at www.ImAnAspie.com and sending me an e-mail.

Thank you so much for allowing me to share my thoughts with you. Life is short and there is so much to learn. Live to learn but not to know and you will always continue to grow. May your life lead you to the place where dreams and reality meet.

With All My Love And Respect,

Brian R. King

About The Author

Brian R. King is a Licensed Clinical Social Worker. Brian's private practice is located in Naperville, IL. Brian brings a unique, threefold perspective to the world of Asperger's. Brian has two sons diagnosed on the Autism Spectrum, Brian works exclusively with Asperger clients and their families, and Brian is also blessed with Asperger's himself.

Brian has become known worldwide for his positive approach to living the Asperger's experience. Brian continuously dedicates his time to serving as an Ambassador between the Asperger and Neurotypical communities. The primary goal is to help both communities learn to effectively communicate, appreciate, and cooperate with each other in a spirit of mutual respect.

www.ingramcontent.com/pod-product-compliance
Lightning Source LLC
Chambersburg PA
CBHW020516100426
42813CB00030B/3273/J